The Living Sea

Ritchard Read

Illustrated by Prudence Theobalds

Explorer 11   **Puffin Books**

PUFFIN BOOKS:
A Division of Penguin Books Ltd
Harmondsworth, Middlesex, England
Penguin Books Inc., 7110 Ambassador Road,
Baltimore, Maryland 21207, U.S.A.
Penguin Books Australia Ltd, Ringwood,
Victoria, Australia

First published 1974

Made and printed in Great Britain by
Westerham Press Ltd, Westerham, Kent
Set in Monophoto Ehrhardt

The Kingdom of the Sea

If you look at a globe of the world some blue is always visible. All the blue is the 'kingdom of the sea' known to the ancient Greeks as 'Oceanus'. It is from the word Oceanus that we get ocean; the vast body of water covering the surface of the globe and geographically divided into the five great oceans, the Pacific, Atlantic, Indian, Arctic and Antarctic. The 'sea' is part of this water but is different from the oceans as it has certain land limits or washes a particular coast, and it is given a proper name such as Red, Mediterranean, North, Irish or Adriatic, etc.

The surface of the earth is 197,000,000 square miles (510,000,000 sq. km) of which 139,000,000 (361,000,000 sq. km) are water and only 58,000,000 (149,000,000 sq. km) are land. If these vast surfaces were laid out flat, the proportion of land to water would be that of the white to the black in the diagram. The seas and oceans (black) account for 71 per cent and the land (white) for 29 per cent of the earth's surface. The total amount of water is 324,000,000 cubic miles (1,370,000,000 cubic km) lying in great hollow basins in the earth's crust. Much of the water is over 12,000 feet (3,657 m or 2,000 fathoms*) deep enough to cover Mount Snowdon more than three and a half times.

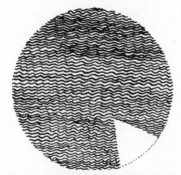

The proportion of sea to land on Earth

*The word 'fathom' is a nautical term used by sailors to measure depth. When a sailing ship made its way into an uncharted area a sailor would 'sound' the water below the ship. He would cast a weighted line forward and let it run through his hands until it touched bottom. He would then quickly pull the line up and measure out the part that was wet in arm lengths or 'stretches'. It is from this that the word fathom is derived. It is thought to have originated from the Danish word 'favn' or German 'faden', both words translated as 'arms extended'. Later, pieces of ribbon, as well as leather, bunting and various knots were incorporated into the line to enable the leadsman to gauge the depth of water more accurately. The fathom as a unit of measurement is now standardized as equal to 6 feet or 1.83 m. The abbreviation for fathom is f or fm.

Overleaf: *The floor of the Pacific Ocean*

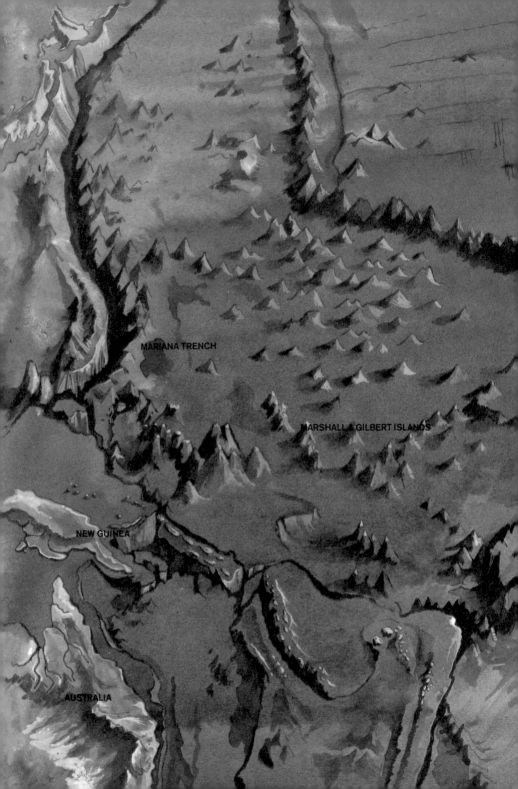

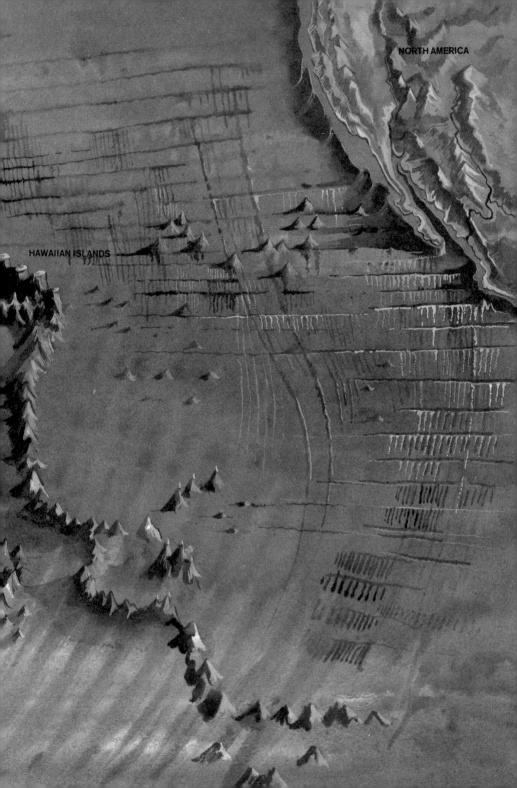

NORTH AMERICA

HAWAIIAN ISLANDS

On the sea floor are great chasms, mountains, valleys, ridges and trenches. Some of the trenches are far deeper than any of those on land. There are also volcanoes many of which are now inactive but some of which are still very much alive. Submarine volcanoes have helped to form and shape the floors of the seas and oceans. In some areas there are elevations of the floor called 'seamounts' which are large submerged islands standing on their own or are mountain chains of dead volcanoes. In the Pacific Ocean there are more than 10,000 volcanoes, many of which have never pushed above the surface. Those that have risen above the water have become the beautiful tropical islands of the South Seas such as Hawaii, Fiji and Samoa. About 800 miles south east of Tahiti in the Pacific, an active submarine volcano has recently been discovered. It rises some 10,000 feet (3,050 m) above the floor of the ocean but its summit is still about 2,000 feet (610 m) below the surface. Whether it will eventually reach the surface only time will tell. Atolls and coral islands form on the sides of volcanoes which have sunk back into the sea or whose tops have been worn away by the sea and weather.

In this great mass of water, from the surface down to the greatest depths, lives an infinite variety of beautiful, strange and fascinating creatures.

Throughout the nineteenth century, naturalists were devoting a great deal of time to learning about the seas and oceans. They wanted to know what lay on the bottom; what it was made of and, more than anything, if there was any form of life there. They were particularly anxious to find out about life in the ocean depths where no life-giving light has ever penetrated and where the inhabitants have to bear a weight of over three tons per square inch on their body surface.

It was not until the famous *Challenger* expedition of 1873–6 under C. Wyville Thomson and William B. Carpenter that definite proof was obtained of life in the depths of the ocean. This expedition was the greatest and most important voyage of deep-sea exploration that Britain had ever undertaken. Thomson and Carpenter travelled nearly 70,000 miles through the seas and oceans of the world, made hundreds of dredgings, and collected

C. Wyville Thomson

living creatures from over 18,000 feet (5,486 m; 3,000 fms) deep. The vast amount of scientific information gathered on this voyage laid the foundation of the science of Oceanography or science of the ocean. The *Challenger* brought back 4,417 kinds of creatures showing that the oceans teemed with all manner of life. All these new, unknown creatures had to be named, studied and classified, which involved a tremendous amount of work and kept scientists busy for many years. All the information was gathered together and published in fifty thick volumes which, if you wanted to buy them today, would cost £1,379.

The Challenger

Since the days of the *Challenger* expedition, marine scientists or oceanographers have explored some very great depths in the oceans.

Between Japan and the Philippine Islands to the south of Guam lies the deepest hole in the oceans, the 'Challenger Deep' in the Mariana Trench. This deep hole in the crust of the earth is 36,198 feet, or nearly seven miles (11,033 m; 6,033 fms), below the surface of the sea. The whole of Mount Everest could be buried in it with room to spare. On 23 January 1960, Lt Don Walsh, US Navy and Jacques Piccard went down into the Mariana Trench in the bathyscaphe *Trieste*. After a hazardous five-hour journey, the *Trieste* and its two passengers gently settled on the bottom of the Challenger Deep. They had conquered the greatest depth on earth. The journey had been undertaken for two reasons. Firstly, to obtain information about diving to great depths and, secondly, to see if there was any form of life at this depth. Realizing that the bathyscaphe would frighten away any inhabitant, Piccard and

The Mariana Trench – the deepest chasm in the oceans

Saipan   Guam

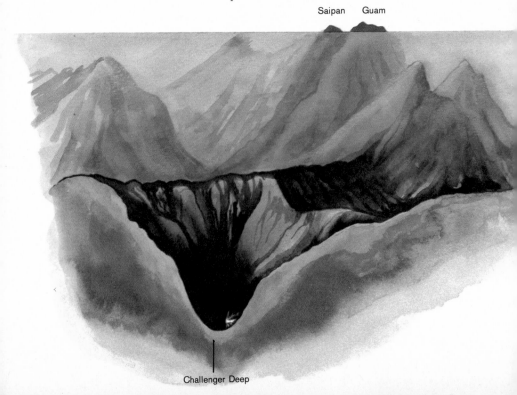

Challenger Deep

Walsh lost no time. They immediately turned on *Trieste*'s powerful searchlight and peered through the thick plastic porthole. Imagine their surprise and excitement when there, right below the porthole, they saw a large fish! Piccard described it in these words, 'Slowly, very slowly, this fish – apparently of the sole family – about a foot long and half as wide, moved away from us, swimming half in the bottom ooze, and disappeared into the black night.' Piccard and Walsh proved beyond doubt that it is possible for life to exist in the greatest depths yet known.

Life in the Sea

To understand how life is possible in the sea we must go back and see what happens at the surface. It is only in the last 150 years or so that naturalists have been interested in the way animals and plants live under natural conditions. This interest has given rise to a new branch of science called **Ecology**. Animals and plants, collectively known as **organisms**, live in close association with their surroundings or **environment**. Over millions of years organisms have developed or evolved ways to adjust or adapt themselves to their environment. A salt-water fish has become adapted to a marine environment and a mouse to a land environment. Although certain organisms are widely distributed throughout a particular environment they do not occupy all of it. They are usually only found in some part of it, the place where they find conditions most suitable for survival. This is called their **habitat**. Ecology then, is the study of organisms in relation to their environment and the way the environment affects organisms in their habitats.

The relationship between an organism and its habitat is important. It takes very little to upset a habitat. A small rise or fall in temperature beyond certain limits, or a change in the salt content (salinity) or composition of the water in a marine environment can make a habitat unsuitable. When this happens on a large scale, and if it is spread over a long time, it causes untold harm to the inhabitants. It may even destroy a habitat completely. This applies particularly to creatures living on the seashore. The big freeze of 1962–3 caused the death of many seashore creatures, in some places the numbers were reduced to one tenth of their usual numbers. By 1965 many of the inhabitants were recovering and were starting to re-establish themselves.

A more serious problem is pollution. Pollution in any form is harmful to organisms, oil and poisonous chemicals being by far the worst. All kinds of pollution find their way into the sea, and are affecting not only coastal areas but far out in the oceans. Thor Heyerdahl in his papyrus reed boat *Ra 1* ran into such polluted ocean water that he and his crew were not able to wash in the water around the boat, and, more recently, reports have come in of large numbers of oil blobs floating about in the ocean in company with all kinds of unsinkable polythene containers.

A typical polluted beach

A disaster like the wrecking of the oil tanker *Torrey Canyon* off the coast of Cornwall in 1967, caused tremendous damage to the beaches and marine life of the seashore. A lot of damage is also caused by small oil slicks that are washed up every day onto the shore from leaks and the washings from tankers. Some slicks and spills have been so serious that they have wiped out most of the sea life and destroyed many habitats in some areas. The sea has been over-used as a general dustbin for sewage, pesticides, industrial waste and general rubbish. Traces of DDT have been found in all the oceans; from inside penguins in the Antarctic to mackerel off the coast of California. The time has come when pollution must stop, before the sea becomes a lifeless cesspool.

The Sea's Green Pastures

The whole cycle of life in the sea, like that on land, depends on the light and warmth of the sun. All life in the sea begins at, or just below, the surface. There, in the light and heat, lives a vast multitude of plants and animals; the **plankton**, that drifts and wanders through the water at the mercy of wind, tides and currents. Plankton is made up of minute floating animals and plants which, on occasion, by their sheer numbers, colour the water brown, green or blood-red. The *plants* are collectively known as **phytoplankton** and the *animals* as **zooplankton**.

Phytoplankton is a large group of one-celled plants that live close to the surface of the water and provide the basic food supply for every animal in the sea, from the lowest sponge to the largest whale. In the spring and early summer, phytoplankton is most abundant, producing great 'bloomings' of the microscopic plants. At such times the water becomes a rich deep green just like some

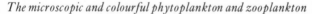

The microscopic and colourful phytoplankton and zooplankton

lush pasture or meadow, which is why phytoplankton is called the 'grass of the sea'.

The minute phytoplankton plants are the staple diet of thousands of zooplankton animals. There are two distinct groups of animals which make up zooplankton, the 'permanent' and the 'temporary' members. Permanent zooplankton animals spend all their life wandering and floating about, and breed, hatch, grow and mature as individuals of the zooplankton. The temporary zooplankton members, on the other hand, are unhatched, floating eggs and the larvae of fishes, crabs and lobsters as well as many other creatures. These spend only a short part of their life in the plankton. Temporary zooplankton larvae grow, become adults and, either settle on the bottom or swim away to be replaced by other, later-developing larvae.

Permanent zooplankton animals are constantly renewed by young ones replacing those eaten by larger animals (predators), or those that die of old age or other causes and a very similar thing happens with phytoplankton. At certain times a particular plant is abundant and widespread. Later, when it reaches its peak of blooming and dies off, some other plant takes over and dominates the scene. In summer, in some coastal areas of America, phytoplankton plants reproduce and increase so much that they actually poison the sea. Waste substances from the plants kill thousands of fishes and other creatures, and the poisonous substances from the water even get blown inland causing sore throats and inflamed eyes amongst the people who live near the coast.

The Mystery of Vertical Migration

In the early days of oceanography naturalists were puzzled by the way plankton behaved in the sea.

When they trawled their nets through the water in daylight they found that most of the catch consisted of phytoplankton, but trawling at night the nets brought up a large number of zooplankton animals. This strange and, as yet, little understood behaviour of the zooplankton is known as 'vertical migration'. The animals change their position upwards and downwards through the water in time with the rising and setting of the sun, and this movement can be followed by sampling the water at various depths at different times. Plankton does not migrate but stays close to the surface day and night.

Another curious thing is that zooplankton animals migrate to different depths. Some go down to about 150 feet (46 m; 25 fms), others stay in shallower water around 60–80 feet (18–24 m; 10–14 fms). At night they return to the surface in an orderly manner, each kind taking its turn. One explanation of the migration is that the water at the surface moves faster than deep water, and by sinking during the day, the animals avoid being carried away from their feeding grounds. The phytoplankton stock is renewed all the time, and when the animals return at night, they find fresh plants on which to feed. But the real reason for vertical migration remains one of the mysteries of the sea.

The daily migration of zooplankton

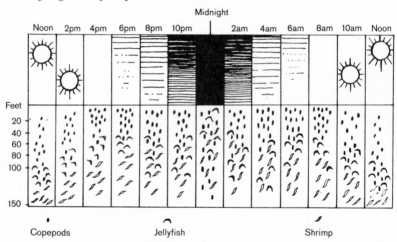

Grass of the Green Pastures

All living creatures need food in some form or another to remain alive. It is from food that we obtain the energy to grow and do all the things we are capable of. Organisms obtain their basic food materials in two ways. They can either manufacture it themselves

14

or they eat it ready made. This is the difference between animals and plants.

Animals are **consumers** and need organic, ready-made food which they obtain by eating other animals or plants.

Green plants are **primary producers** and, by means of a very important and special substance called **chlorophyll**, they manufacture their own basic foods. They use energy from the sun to convert simple, chemical substances into more complex materials which become their food. The manufacturing process is called **photosynthesis** or 'building with light'.

The upper layers of the sea receive all the light and necessary mineral salts to promote the growth of phytoplankton plants. In the spring, early summer and, for a short time in early autumn, phytoplankton 'bloomings' form acres of green pastures over vast areas of the sea. When the sea turns to a deep rich green it becomes the feeding ground of a great variety of consumers, attracting large numbers of zooplankton animals to the area followed by the bigger consumers, the fishes.

The most common and abundant phytoplankton plants are **diatoms**. Diatoms are microscopic, one-celled plants enclosed in an elaborately sculptured, transparent glass-like box of silica. Inside each box is a small blob of living matter containing light-brown or yellowish-green chlorophyll. Silica is a mineral that diatoms extract from the water to form their box-like shell. The shell is in two parts fitting together like the top and bottom of a pill-box. They are rounded, triangular, oval or pencil-shaped, and some form chains or lattices with spiny projections of great beauty. Pits, grooves, ridges and perforations on the outside of the boxes form intricate patterns and by these patterns we know that there are over 9,000 different kinds of diatoms.

Diatoms are the most important food supply in the sea. Each one is a tiny chemical factory using the sunlight to convert mineral salts into foodstuffs. Diatoms do the same job in the sea as grass does on land. Most marine animals, from the smallest shrimp to the largest whale, either directly or indirectly, depend on diatoms for food.

The Arctic and Antarctic oceans are the true homes of diatoms.

Overleaf: *A food web*

15

During the short polar spring and summer the sea warms up with plenty of sunlight for photosynthesis and the water is full of mineral fertilizers. It is then that diatoms grow and multiply so quickly that the water turns into a rich, nourishing phytoplankton soup. The Antarctic is the richest feeding ground of all the oceans, with diatoms forming 99 per cent of the phytoplankton.

Diatoms

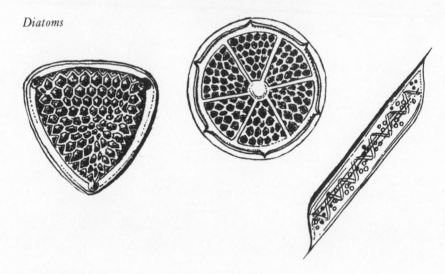

The Chain of Life

Like the links in a chain, animals and plants depend one upon the other for their food. Many zooplankton animals provide a direct link between phytoplankton and the larger marine animals by what is called a **food chain**. A food chain always starts with plants, **the primary producers**, the first link in the chain. The second link is formed by a plant eating animal or **herbivore**. Link three is formed by the herbivore being eaten by a flesh-eater or **carnivore**. The first carnivore is usually a bit larger than the herbivore it consumes. The carnivore, in turn, becomes food for a second one which then falls prey to a third. So the cycle goes on until all the links in the chain are joined. A food chain is a matter of eat-and-be-eaten in which the energy from the food is transferred first, from plants to animals and then from animal to animal. Some food chains which involve only a few creatures are quite simple; others, where many kinds of individuals take part, are more complicated and known as **food webs**.

One of the more abundant and successful diatom feeders are the **copepods**. Copepods are small shrimp-like organisms and form the largest group in the permanent zooplankton. Rarely any bigger than a grain of rice, they probably outnumber all other creatures on earth. There are about 10,000 different kinds of copepods living in the sea. Some feed solely on plants, others are carnivores feeding on small animals, and some obtain their food from all manner of waste matter. One particular kind of copepod is called '*Calanus finmarchicus*', and measures about a quarter of an inch (5 mm) long with six pairs of swimming legs and two long, jointed feelers or antennae on the head. The mouth is surrounded by bristles which are kept rapidly in motion. The movement of the bristles helps to keep calanus afloat and at the same time produces a current of water. As the water passes through the bristles diatoms and any other food material is sieved out and passed into the mouth. *Calanus finmarchicus* is the main food of the common herring, one of the most numerous fishes in the sea. The cod, a larger fish, eats the herring and the seal feeds on the cod. The last link in this particular food chain is the killer whale that feeds on the seal. The killer whale is the last link because it is not eaten by any other creature. Its only enemy is man who, in many cases, forms the final link where animals of commercial value or 'sport' are concerned.

Closely associated with food chains is the 'food pyramid'. The chain showed that the transfer of energy from food takes place between progressively larger animals. An increase in size of the animal at each link means that the larger the animal the less chance there is of it being eaten by another. It also means that food becomes scarcer and more difficult to find. The animal has to use up a lot of energy in its search for food. This activity leaves only a small amount of energy for growth, breeding and all the other things animals do, so there is always a far greater number of creatures at

A food pyramid: (from top to bottom) man – killer whale – seal – cod – herring – calanus finmarchicus – plankton

the bottom of a pyramid than at the top. A pyramid starting with 1,000 lb (454 kg) of diatoms provides food for 100 lb (45.4 kg) of zooplankton animals. These produce 10 lb (4.5 kg) of food for herrings, which in turn, provide 1 lb (454 g) of food for the cod. So from this you can see that there is a reduction of about one-tenth at each stage in the links of a food chain, and why the bigger animals have such enormous appetites.

The World of Land and Water

The seashore is one of the most colourful and fascinating habitats. Its inhabitants live in a narrow world between land and water, and can be seen twice a day when exposed by the outgoing tide. The plants and animals of the tidal or **littoral** zone of the shore live in

Seaweeds: (left to right) serrated wrack – knotted wrack – bladder wrack – channelled wrack – thongweed – oarweed – one of the red seaweeds

one of the seas most dangerous environments. Every day they are exposed to the air or are covered by the tides. During storms they are pounded and pulled about by the waves; sand and stones scour them, often causing great damage. Fresh water from rain, rivers and streams invades their territory; and ice, snow and cold winds kill many of them. The tidal zone is one of the sea's harshest environments.

But, like all other creatures they have adapted to withstand all the normal dangers and hazards. Through evolution they have learnt how to meet and deal with the conditions of their environment, though they have still to find a way of dealing with pollution.

The Seashore

All seashores differ in their outline, extent and the way they are made. Some consist of rocks, boulders, shingles; others have shingles with sand at low tide; some are all sand.

Every shore is different and in each littoral, or tidal, area live different kinds of inhabitants. The shape of the coastline and the depth of water off the coast determine how high and how low the tides will come up the beach. In some parts of the world the range of the tides is very small. In the Mediterranean and parts of the Baltic, the difference between high and low water is only about two feet (609 mm). In the Bay of Fundy, in Canada, the water may rise more than fifty feet (15 metres) above low-tide mark. Life in the tidal zone is influenced by the comings and goings of the tides. The plants and animals must have water at all times. Many follow the outgoing tide and return when the water comes in again. Others seek refuge in rock pools, or under stones, rocks or seaweeds. Those that are unable to move like mussels, and barnacles, simply retain enough water in their shells until the sea returns. Some, like the limpet, cling hard to the rocks and seal themselves down.

What sort of living things can we expect to find on a typical seashore? On a rocky shore, the most obvious are the large, brown seaweeds which drape themselves over the rocks. Seaweeds belong to a large group of plants known as the **algae**. They have no flowers, or real leaves, or roots. The more outstanding of the brown seaweeds are the various kinds of **wracks**. Wracks distribute themselves in a rocky littoral zone according to the height of the tides, and are usually found in the following order. The first to be uncovered, or highest up on the beach, is the **channelled** wrack followed by the **flat, knotted** and, then, lowest on the shore, the **serrated** wrack. Many other kinds of seaweeds are found on the seashore, the **oar-weed, laminaria** and **thong-weed**, all of which live in the water below low-tide level, but are exposed when the water is extremely low. There are also many smaller seaweeds recognized by their characteristic colours, the green, blue-green and red seaweeds, but these are never as conspicuous as the large, brown weeds. Seaweeds are important to shore life, as they provide food for a number of animals, as well as hiding-places where they can find refuge from the sun and wind.

There is no better way of seeing the life of the seashore than to follow an outgoing tide. On the rocks, as the water goes down, you see the first of the larger, easily distinguished animals, the **barnacles** and **limpets**. At first sight you might think that these two are related, that one is the young, undeveloped form of the other. But this is not so. The shape is roughly the same, and they both stick firmly to the rocks, but if you look carefully, you will find many differences.

The limpet has a large, thick, brownish-green, domed, smooth conical shell in one piece.

The barnacle is smaller with a white or greyish, rough, but also conical, shell, like a miniature volcano, separated into several pieces

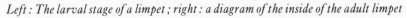

Left : The larval stage of a limpet ; right : a diagram of the inside of the adult limpet

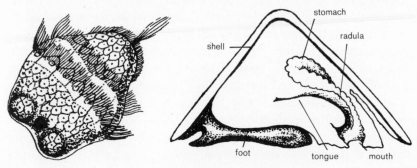

Barnacles and limpets. The scars on the rocks show where limpets once settled. The scars fit the limpet shells exactly

or compartments. The top of the barnacle shell is open, and the opening is protected by four small valves surrounded by the sharp, pointed projections of the compartments. It is these points which dig into and cut your feet if you walk barefoot over rocks and boulders on the shore. Limpets belong to a large group of snail-like animals, the gastropods (or stomach footed), the same group as the common garden snail. Limpets stick to the rocks with a large, strong, muscular sucking disc, called a 'foot'. The foot is really the limpet's ventral or stomach surface from which the word gastropod is derived. Limpets are plant feeders and browse, when covered by water at high tide, by rasping small algae off the rock with a special tongue called a 'radula'. The radula is a horny ribbon covered with rows of small, sharp, hooked teeth. The ribbon and teeth are moved backwards and forwards like pulling a rope over a pulley. The teeth rapidly wear away but they are as rapidly replaced by new ones continuously forming at the lower end of the ribbon.

Limpets can loosen their grip on the rock. They glide over the surface of the rock on their foot and go searching for food. Although

24

limpets never have to wander far for their food, they always return to their permanent place on the same rock. This constant settling in the same place leaves a scar in the rock, which exactly fits the outline of the shell. Limpets are 'bisexual' organisms – there are males and females. But limpets reproduce in a different way to other gastropods. The female lays her eggs one at a time, in the water, where they are fertilized by sperm from the male, which is also shed in the water. The young limpet hatches from the egg as a larva known as a **trocophore** and spends about ten days floating as plankton. It then sinks and is washed towards the shore where it settles on some convenient rock and turns into the common shore limpet.

Barnacles, or cirripedia, belong to a totally different group. They are crustaceans (shellfish), one of the largest groups in the animal kingdom. Barnacles, unlike limpets, can never move from a place where they once settle and become attached. They remain permanently fixed to whatever surface they settle on, rocks, bits of wood, the bottom of ships, even glass bottles. How then, do they get their food and reproduce? Nearly everything a barnacle does is in some way complicated and specialized. Barnacles gather food from the water by pushing their legs out though the opening at the top of the shell. When the legs are in the water, they uncurl and lock together by means of small hair-like projections and spines to form a kind of catch net. This net collects diatoms and any other floating material from the water. When enough food has been gathered, the legs are quickly drawn back into the shell and the food is passed into the large mouth cone.

The way barnacles reproduce is rather complicated too. In nearly all crustaceans there are two sexes, male and female, but barnacles have both male and female reproductive organs and are known as **hermaphrodites**. Under normal conditions, however, fertilization takes place by the transfer of the male sperm to the female eggs from one individual to another. The eggs are fertilized inside the shell and hatch into small larvae – the **nauplii**. As the nauplii hatch they are squirted out of the shell into the water where they form part of the plankton. They grow and cast their skin several times and change shape completely. From the roughly

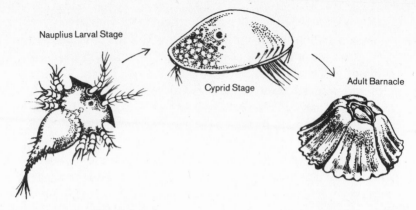

The development of the barnacle

triangular shape with frontal horns and one central eye of the nauplii, they take on the shape of a tiny mussel – the **cyprid**. The body of the cyprid is enclosed in two minute hinged transparent shells through which the legs and antennae or feelers protrude. The single eye of the nauplius stage is replaced by two eyes, one on each side of the head and can easily be seen through the shell.

The cyprid stage is critical in the life of a shore-living or acorn barnacle. As a member of the plankton family cyprids run the risk of being carried far from the shore by wind, tides and currents. They stay for only a short time in the upper layers of the water then gradually sink to the bottom. If they fall onto a rock or other hard surface they find a suitable place in which to settle, usually a small pit, ridge or some roughness of the surface. As barnacles like to crowd together cyprids often settle close to or on other barnacles. Once a suitable place is found, the cyprids hold on to the spot with their feelers. Then, with a special fluid produced from inside the feelers, they cement themselves in place. Once attached, they pull themselves down onto the feelers, turn on their backs and come to rest with their legs pointing upwards. The two cyprid shells are cast off, the eyes disappear and the true barnacle shell begins to form. In about a month the shell is completely formed and hardens as a protective home for the animal.

These are just two examples of the life histories of small but easily recognizable seashore animals that live in a littoral or tidal area.

Fishes and Mammals

Stretching seawards from the shore, beyond low-water mark, the land slopes gently downwards forming a platform, the 'continental shelf'. All large continents and most islands have continental shelves varying in extent and depth. The British Isles rest on a shelf 300 feet (91 m; 50 fms) deep and stretches for about 200 miles (322 km) westwards from the Cornish coast to the English Channel and North Sea. It then turns northwards and borders many coasts of continental Europe.

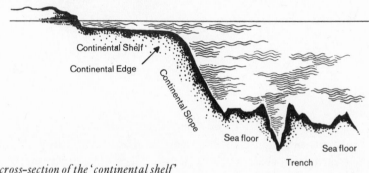

A cross-section of the 'continental shelf'

Off the eastern coasts of South America and parts of North America, the continental shelf is only about a mile wide. The land then plunges more or less straight down into the deep waters of the Pacific Ocean. Most other continents have shelves which extend about 45–50 miles (72–81 km). Continental shelves cover about 10 mil. sq. miles (26 mil. sq. km) of the total area of the oceans.

The water of the continental shelves forms comparatively shallow seas reaching a depth of about 450 feet (137 m; 75 fms). It is these waters, teeming with fish, which are so important to the fishing industry. Here, a great variety of fishes of all kinds move freely through the water and journey to their breeding grounds. This free-swimming 'pelagic' life is different in many parts of the world. It includes most of the valuable 'commercial' or 'fish-

'Commercial' fish : (top to bottom) whiting, mackerel, sprats, haddock, cod

mongers' fishes and also squids, seals, sharks and whales. The floor of the continental shelf, with its gentle hills and depressions, is the home of innumerable creatures that settle on or in the sand, mud or gravel on the bottom.

Fishes, during their evolution, have developed into beautifully shaped, graceful animals ideally suited to underwater life. With their streamlined shape, they can swim rapidly after prey and escape their enemies. As with all other animals, fishes prefer certain regions in which to live and occupy different habitats, from the upper layers of the sea down to the greatest depths.

Fishes are separated into two groups, the 'pelagic' and 'demersal'. A pelagic fish spends nearly all its adult life in mid-water between the surface and the bottom while a demersal fish stays on or near the bottom most of the time. There are times, however, when a pelagic fish, such as the herring, will spend some time close to the bottom and a demersal fish, like the cod, will swim up to the surface.

The fishing industry studies the habits of fishes to find out where and how to fish. Fishing for pelagic fishes is usually done by 'drifting' from a boat called a 'drifter'. When the drifter reaches a good fishing ground, the crew play out or 'shoot' about three miles (5 km) of line. Attached to the line is a series of nets about fifty feet (15 m) square supported by glass, metal or plastic floats. When the 'fleet' of nets has been shot, the drifter stops engines and drifts over the area with the wind and tide. It is known that pelagic fishes closely follow the movement of zooplankton animals and so the best catches of fish are made at night. The fishes rise with the zooplankton and get caught in the suspended nets.

Demersal fishes are caught from a 'trawler' from which is lowered onto the sea bed, a large, weighted, bag-like net, the 'trawl'. The trawl is dragged slowly along the bottom and sweeps up any fish in its path. There are other ways of catching both pelagic and demersal fishes, but drifting and trawling are used extensively on the continental shelf.

The Herring

Around the British Isles, off the coasts of the continent and in many other parts of the world, the herring is one of the most common and abundant pelagic fishes. It is the most important of all food fishes in the sea. Its nearest relatives are the pilchards and sprats. The herring is easily distinguished by its shimmering blue-green back and silvery flanks. Herrings crowd together in large shoals, a form of protection where there is safety in numbers. Should one of the herrings in the shoal be singled out by a predator, the whole shoal scatters in a split second. The predator is left with one fish to chase while all the other herrings swim to safety. When the danger has passed, the shoal reforms and goes on its way.

Nearly all female pelagic and demersal fishes produce eggs that float. The herring is an exception as its eggs are heavier than water and sink to the bottom as soon as they are laid. Covered by a very sticky substance as they are produced, the eggs stick to anything they touch. A female herring can produce from 10,000 to 30,000 eggs at each spawning. Millions of herrings, all spawning at the

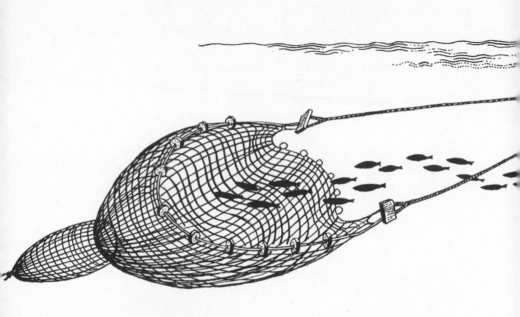

Two methods of fishing: trawling (left) and drifting (right)

same time in the same breeding ground, cover the sea bed and everything on it in great sheets of sticky eggs. Up to 500,000,000 herrings have been known to assemble over the same breeding ground at the same time. Shoals nine miles (14.5 km) long and two to three miles (3.2–5 km) wide have been recorded.

'Flat' fishes

Plaice, flounders and soles are demersal fishes of great commercial value. The commonest of these around the British Isles is the plaice. Plaice produce eggs that float and a female can lay as many as 500,000 at once. The eggs are spawned in mid-winter in the Flemish Bight half way between the mouth of the Thames and the coast of Holland. As many as 60,000,000 plaice gather in this

30

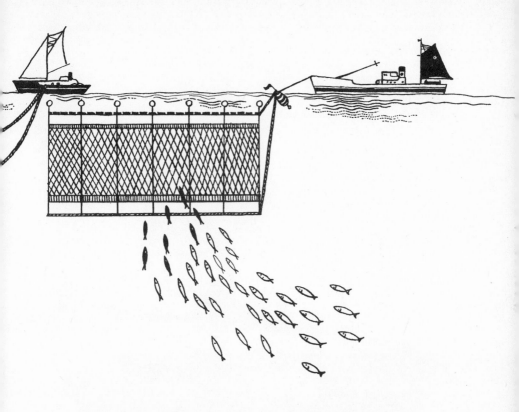

area and lay their eggs over the deep waters of the Bight. For a
short while, the eggs float about as temporary plankton, drifting
with the currents towards what are called 'nursery banks', in
shallower water nearer the coast. The young newly hatched plaice
remain for about a fortnight attached to the egg case and feed on
the rich egg-yolk. After a further eight or nine days, the small
larval fish wriggle free of the egg case and begin feeding on the
smaller kinds of diatoms. As they grow, they start to eat larger
diatoms and some zooplankton animals. During the free-swimming
stage in the plankton, the young plaice is shaped like any normal
looking fish. It is flattened sideways, has a rather large head with
an eye on each side. In another fifteen days, however, the whole
fish undergoes a startling change. It now becomes flattened and
rounded like a pancake. The eye from the left side moves across

the top of the head and joins the one on the right. When these changes have taken place, the young plaice, now about three-quarters of an inch (20 mm) long, settle on the bottom and begin life as demersal fishes.

Plaice grow rather slowly, and when a year old they are still only about 3 inches (76 mm) long, but at five years old they can measure 14 inches (355 mm). The mature fish lies on the bottom on its stomach which is really its left side, with the right side, its back, uppermost. The underpart is silvery white and the top is dark with small red spots. The body is surrounded by a continuous fin in two parts stretching from just behind the head to the tail. The plaice

Herring and plaice

swims by 'undulating its flat body in a series of waves passing from head to tail and so skims horizontally forward like a billowing magic carpet.' It swims in short bursts just above the sea bed and, after each 'take off', gently glides back onto the bottom. Then, with its fins, it throws up sand and small pebbles onto its back. At the same time it wriggles its body into the sand or gravel. In this way, plaice and other flat fishes hide from their enemies by merging with the background. They can, like the chameleon, change colour to match their surroundings. They do this by means of special cells under the skin called **chromatophores.** The chromatophores lie under the top transparent scales and contain, red, orange, yellow and black pigment. By contracting and expanding the chromatophores, the plaice can change the colour of skin to look like sand, gravel or any other natural surface on which it settles.

How a plaice develops

Marine mammals

Marine mammals, like those on land, are warm-blooded animals, bear their young alive and rear them on milk. The adults depend on the sea for food and can spend long periods in and under the water, but must return to the surface to breathe. Most marine mammals, except whales and certain kinds of seals, come back on to the land to have their pups. Seals, sea-lions and walruses are known as **pinnipeds** or fin-footed. Their bodies are streamlined and they are fast and agile swimmers. Under the skin they have a thick layer of fat called 'blubber'. Blubber is a reserve of food on which the animal draws when food is scarce. It is also an insulator against cold and helps the animal to float.

Pinnipeds are found in the Arctic and Antarctic seas; some extend beyond the polar circles into Canada, Greenland and Iceland in the north. Isolated colonies of the grey seal live and breed

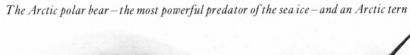

The Arctic polar bear – the most powerful predator of the sea ice – and an Arctic tern

on the Farne Islands off the coast of Northumberland in England. Some of the south polar seals range as far as the Galapagos Islands. The different kinds of pinnipeds have different feeding habits and feed on fish, penguins and other sea birds and squids. The Antarctic 'crab-eater' seal, for all its name, does not feed on crabs but on a large kind of plankton animal called 'krill'.

The Arctic is the home of the fearsome polar bear. It lives on the northern pack ice and is the most powerful mammal predator of the sea ice. A full-grown male polar bear can weigh 1,600 lb (726 kg) and measure up to 11 feet (over 3 m) in height. Polar bears feed mainly on seals which they stalk across the ice when the seals are basking. So strong and powerful is the polar bear that it can drag a 200-lb (90-kg) seal from its breathing hole in the ice. When seals are scarce it will feed off birds eggs, fish, seaweeds and any kind of refuse it can get. In the summer, when the bears come on land to moult they eat lichens, grass, berries and anything they can uproot.

Whales, the true marine mammals, never come on to the land. They spend all their time in the water and are the giant mammals of the sea. There are two kinds of whales, those with teeth and those in which the teeth have been replaced by 'whalebones' or 'baleens'. There are only ten kinds of baleen whales and seventy-four kinds with teeth.

The blue whale is a baleen whale and is the largest animal that has ever lived on earth. It can grow to over 100 feet (30 m) long and weigh up to 140 tons (142 tonnes) which is about the same weight as thirty elephants. It is sometimes called the 'sulphur' bottom whale because of the heavy growth of diatoms that cover its belly and make it look yellow.

Blue whales live in and around the Antarctic circle where the main food supply is found. The whales' feeding habits show how important plankton is as food for marine animals. If you look back to the food pyramid on page 20 you will recall that each link in the food chain reduces the amount of food and energy. Most of the food

Overleaf: *The Pinnipeds – including the walrus, the sea lion, the fur seal, the ringed seal, the leopard seal, and the elephant seal*

is at the bottom of the pyramid where the greatest number of organisms are found. Now a blue whale with its tremendous size cannot waste energy chasing its food, so, to satisfy its large appetite, it reduces the number of links in its food chain. It gets as close as possible to the greatest supply, the bottom of the pyramid, and does it by using only two links. The first link consists of phyto-plankton, the second is a 2 to $2\frac{1}{2}$ inches (51–64 mm) long, shrimp-like animal, the 'krill'. This particular food chain, phytoplankton – krill – baleen whales, is the shortest chain in the oceans.

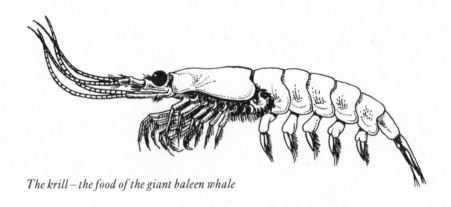

The krill – the food of the giant baleen whale

The Antarctic krill, *Euphausia superba*, like all other krill, is a herbivore that feeds on diatoms. Krill is sometimes so abundant in the Antarctic that the water appears red from the pigment inside the krills' thin, transparent shell.

Instead of teeth all baleen whales have a sort of strainer of flexible, horny plates with fringed edges – the 'baleens' or 'whale bones'. There are from 250 to 500 plates arranged in rows about a half-inch apart hanging from the roof of the mouth. The hair-like fringes form a sieve through which krill is strained from the water. Baleen whales gulp masses of krill and sea water as they swim along. The water is forced out through the plates and the sides of the mouth by the tongue but the krill is caught up in the fringes, and from there it is passed into the gullet and swallowed. It is believed that blue whales feed for just six months during the Antarctic

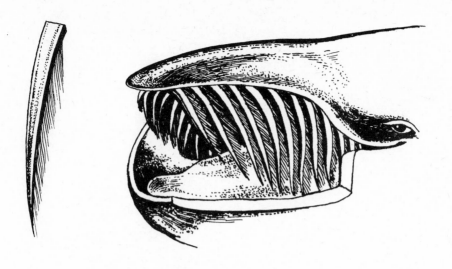

The mouth of a whale showing the baleen plates, and a close up of a baleen plate

spring and summer. With the coming of colder, winter weather, when there is less krill available, the whales move northwards to warmer waters to bear their young. At this time the whales go without food and live off the accumulated 'blubber' which they built up during the spring and summer. A large blue whale needs two or three tonnes of krill a day to sustain its enormous bulk; so feeding at this rate for about 183 days, one blue whale consumes from 350 to 500 tonnes of krill.

In the past six years about 350,000 blue whales have been slaughtered for their oil. The flesh has been made into fertilizers and food for pets. At present there are only about 1,000 of these majestic creatures left to roam the southern oceans.

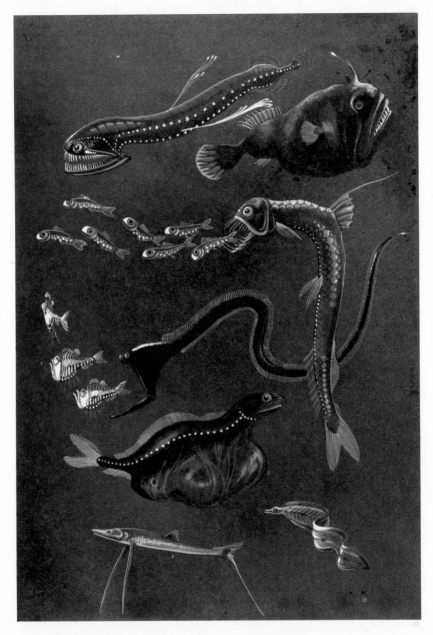

Above: *The fish of the ocean depths – the photostomias quernei, the angler, the lantern, the viper, the gulper eel, the hatchet, the glass eel, and the tripod fish*

Left: *The giants of the oceans – the humped-back whale, the blue whale, the killer whale, and the sperm whale*

The Realm of Darkness

The submerged land of the continental shelf ends at the 'continental edge'. From here it plunges steeply downwards as the 'continental slope' to the ocean floor miles below the surface. Here, in a dark, cold and noiseless world live some of the most remarkable creatures. No light from the surface ever reaches these depths but there is a kind of light produced by the animals themselves. More than two-thirds of deep-sea animals produce a type of light known as **'bioluminescence'** or living light. The light is produced by special organs in certain areas of the head and body. It comes from cells and is produced by a chemical reaction. Bioluminescence has many uses in the deep-water world. It is used to attract prey and as recognition signs so that the same kinds of animals are brought together for mating, but it is not known for sure what the real purpose of this light is. It is so well developed in so many deep-sea creatures, however, that it must have some important purpose.

In the depths, food is just as important to the inhabitants as anywhere else. All the food that eventually reaches the bottom originates and comes from the surface. The dying and dead remains of plankton fall as a continuous supply to the ocean floor, supplemented by the carcasses and debris of larger animals that die of old age or wounds and which descend to the bottom as food for scavengers. In recent experiments, baited cameras have been lowered to a depth of 4,600 feet (1,400 m; 766 fms) off the coast of California to see what happens. Many large, active swimming fishes were soon attracted to the bait and were automatically photographed. These experiments have shown that there are far more creatures living at great depths than was at first suspected. Most of the fishes that live in the depths of the sea are small, measuring only a few inches in length. An important deep-sea fish is the 'lantern' fish. About 4–6 inches (101–152 mm) long. Lantern fish live at about 3,500 feet (1,066 m; 583 fms) deep and rise to the surface on dark, moonless nights, to feed on plankton. After feeding they return to the depths, their body full of nourishing plankton, and they are therefore a rich source of food for other creatures.

'Angler' fish live at depths of 11,000 to 12,000 feet (3,353–3,658 m; 1,833–2,000 fms). They have a luminescent lure that dangles from the end of a modified fin ray. The ray projects from the front of the head like a fishing rod. The lure at the end attracts prey towards the mouth which is then caught and swallowed. Angler fish feed on lantern fish, hatchet fish and many invertebrates.

The most remarkable deep-sea fishes are the 'tripod' fishes. These fishes support themselves above the soft ooze of the bottom by raising themselves on three supports. They have two elongated rays from the side or 'pectoral' fins and one ray projecting from the tail. These fishes have been photographed at depths of 35,000 feet (7,010 m; 3,833 fms) perched on their three leg-like stilts. The rays are also used for walking and as feelers to find food.

The modern pioneers of deep-ocean research, like Captain Cousteau, are opening new worlds and revealing many mysteries of the sea. They are slowly solving and coming to understand the life histories of deep-sea creatures and soon there will be permanent ocean-bottom laboratories in which scientists will live and do their experiments and carry on their observations. It is now well established that there is much more life in the deep oceans than was at first thought possible, but still the sea retains many of its mysteries.

A Prehistoric Visitor

Richard Jefferies, in one of his books, says of the sea, 'There is still something in it not quite grasped and understood, something still to be discovered, a mystery!' How true this has turned out to be. Who would have thought that on the 23 December 1938 a 'fishy' bombshell was to explode on the world of science. For this is exactly what happened.

On that particular day, a small trawler fishing at a depth of about 240 feet (73 m; 40 fms) off East London, South Africa, returned to port with her catch. On the deck was a pile of unwanted fishes that had been put aside to be looked over for anything unusual; an arrangement made between the owners of the trawler and a Miss Courtenay-Latimer, curator of the East London Museum. In that pile, Miss Latimer was to discover one of the greatest scientific finds of all times. She found, buried under a mass of other fishes and sharks, one which she had never seen before and realizing that it was something unusual she decided that it was worth keeping. With a great deal of trouble she managed to get the big five-foot (1.5-m), heavy fish back to the museum. She made a drawing and noted some of the fish's peculiarities before sending it to be preserved.

The coelacanth

The drawing and notes were sent to Dr J. L. B. Smith, a prominent and well-known South African ichthyologist (fish specialist). When Dr Smith saw Miss Latimer's drawing, he could not believe his eyes. He spent a long time studying the drawing and consulting reference books, and finally came to the conclusion that what Miss Latimer had found was a coelacanth (seel-a-kanth), a relic from the far-distant past; a fish that had first lived in the sea 300 million years ago; a fish known only from its fossil remains dating 60 to 70 million years when it was thought to have died out. But now, here, in the Museum at East London, was a stuffed, mounted specimen for all to see, a living fossil, a prehistoric visitor.

This remarkable find caused a sensation among scientists all over the world. Many could not believe that such a thing was possible, but had to accept the evidence and authority of Dr Smith's identification. The East London Museum's coelacanth was named *Latimaria chalumnae* in honour of Miss Latimer. The *chalumnae* part of the name is taken from the actual place where the fish was caught, near the mouth of the Chalumna River.

From 1938 to January 1972 more than seventy coelacanths have been caught, all in moderately deep water around the Comores Islands between Madagascar and East Africa.

The recovery of creatures from the depths of the oceans was started by the *Challenger* expedition one hundred years ago. The more recent capture of coelacanths and the dive of the *Trieste* into the Mariana Trench shows that the seas still hold many surprises. Study of the deep ocean, the world of darkness and sparse food, has revealed some of the strangest creatures on earth. Oceanographers will discover many more unusual creatures to fascinate us and raise our hopes for the future of the continuance of life in the sea.

Some Important Deep-Sea Expeditions

1 British expedition, HMS *Erebus* and *Terror*, 1839–43, under Sir James Clark Ross and J. D. Hooker to the Southern Seas of Antarctica. Dredgings made down to 2,400 feet (400 fms) provided many forms of living creatures. All the valuable material collected was later lost to science through neglect.

2 American expedition, under Charles Wilkes and J. D. Dana, 1838–42. Extensive collections were made in many parts of the oceans including an enormous number of fishes which were never reported on.

3 British expedition under R. Fitzroy and Charles Darwin in 1831–6 in HMS *Beagle*. A round-the-world voyage which greatly added to our knowledge of natural history and on which Darwin gathered most of his information for his book *The Origin of Species*.

4 British expedition of the survey ship HMS *Beacon* in 1841 to the Aegean Sea with Edward Forbes as naturalist. Forbes inspired many other naturalists to undertake deep-sea dredgings. He recovered many forms of life from 1,800 feet (300 fms).

5 British expedition of HMS *Lightning* and *Porcupine* in 1868–70 to the North Atlantic and Mediterranean under C. Wyville Thomson and William B. Carpenter. Many new creatures were discovered from dredgings at 12,000 feet (2,000 fms).

6 American expedition of USS *Albatross* from 1888–1905 under the naturalist A. Agassiz. Extensive collections were made over large areas of the Pacific from where many forms of living creatures were found.

7 German expedition of 1889 to the north Atlantic under Professor Victor Hensen in the SS *National*. The main object of this voyage was the study of the wandering, floating microscopic surface life which was named by Hensen, 'plankton'.

8 German deep-sea expedition of 1898–9 of the *Valdivia* to the Atlantic, Indian and Antarctic oceans, under Professor Carl Chun. Many successful dredgings at great depths recovering large, important collections of living creatures.

9 Belgian expedition of the *Belgica* in 1897–9 to the Antarctic, returned with many biological collections from Graham Sound and Peter I island. The *Belgica* was the first ship to spend the winter in the Antarctic.

10 Dutch expedition of the *Siboga* of 1899–1900, known as the Netherlands Deep-Sea Expedition whose main purpose was the study of the deep sea in the East Indies and Malaya.

11 Scottish Antarctic expedition of the *Scotia* in 1902–4, recovered many interesting creatures from deep trawls in the Weddell Sea.

12 Danish expedition *Dana* in 1928–30 sailed round the world and discovered some new kinds of creatures from great depths.

This is in no way a complete list of all the many expeditions and voyages undertaken by various countries in the exploration of the sea. It does, however, give an idea of the tremendous work which has been done and is still being done in the thirst for knowledge and understanding of life in the seas and oceans of the world.

Further Reading

BARRETT, J.H. and YONGE, C.M., *Collins Pocket Guide to the Seashore*, Collins, 1958.
BERRIL, N.J., *The Life of the Ocean*, McGraw-Hill, 1966.
DEACON, G.E.R., *Oceans*, Paul Hamlyn, 1962.
EVANS, I.O., *The Observer's Book of the Sea and Seashore*, Warne & Co. Ltd, 1962.
FRIEDRICH, H., *Marine Biology*, Sidgwick & Jackson, 1969.
HARDY, A., *The Open Sea*, Vol. 1, *The World of Plankton*, New Naturalist Series, Collins, 1956.
HARDY, A., *The Open Sea: Its Natural History*, Vol. 2, *Fishes and Fisheries*, New Naturalist Series, Collins, 1959.
IDYLL, C.P., *Abyss: the Deep Sea and the Creatures that Live in It*, Crowell Company, New York, 1971.
The Fascinating Secrets of Oceans and Islands, The Reader's Digest Association Ltd, 1972.
RYAN, P., *The Ocean World*, Puffin Books & Longman Young Books, 1973.
SMITH, J.L.B., *Old Fourlegs: the Discovery of the Coelacanth*, Pan Books, 1956.
STREET, P., *Between the Tides*, The Scientific Book Club, 1952.
THORSON, G., *Life in the Sea*, World University Library, 1971.

Index